Sincerely Yours

Blushing Poetry
Part I

Sincerely Yours

Blushing Poetry

Part I

R. S. Chaithanya

(As Hansavahini)

EXCELLER BOOKS™
A GLOBAL PRESS

Sincerely Yours
Blushing Poetry–Part I

Cover art by Exceller Books

ISBN: 978-81-19524-58-7

First published in India in 2024 by Exceller Books,
An imprint of GE Group
Address: G1, Dream Apartment, Degree College Road, Belgharia,
Kolkata, 700056, India

EXCELLER BOOKS™
A GLOBAL PRESS

www.excellerbooks.com

For everyone who listens to my words and emotions,
when I need something.

Acknowledgements

Hello, I can't possibly thank everyone who has contributed to this book. Every woman and man who has ever come into my life has played a part. You all know who you are, so in case I missed you out, like always, sorry.

Thanks to My Family, Relatives, Friends, Well-wishers, Teachers & Professors and other writers who helped & improved my writing further and gave opportunities to reach high in the sky. God, for giving me so much.

My readers, for blessing me with so much love. It is because of you that I get to do what I love–tell stories.

Thanks to everyone who ever contributed and loved me & my writings.

Here are my collections of stories and poems based on different genres imported with magic and colors of life from past to present.

I would like to thank at last my favourite lords—Mother Mirra and Sri Aurobindo Ghosh—a better guide and friend forever who I worship as a devotee and seek their blessings, and they are the first readers of all my books.

Preface

It is my pleasure to introduce to you that my latest work of 3rd solo book, which has been crafted yet another masterpiece in the literary world through Anthologies and Awards.

This book is the witness to my dedication to the craft of writing and my passion for exploring the compound themes of earthly existence.

This book's purpose is to provide readers with a thought-provoking narrative that delves into the intricacies of culture and traditions.

Love, as has been recognized all around, is the pith of human existence and the abundant power that satisfies the innovative inclination of the artist, who feels the level of heartfelt inclination brimming with profound force.

This is the justification for why it has been a number one and lethargic topic of verse for ages.

It is pervaded by the writer's straightforwardness, immaculateness of heart, and force of motivation, which are set apart by earnestness, unwaveringness, and innocence.

It is bounteously improved with creative wandering and spinning of reasonableness in the delightful sky of the heart.

In this regard, the female viewpoint on various aspects of love is more essential and often sought after by literary enthusiasts, as I have discovered:

"Unspeakable closeness with each breath together.
Genuine romance is estimated by how profoundly the heart rhymes.
The exciting bends in the road of summer winter times,
Melts and blasts as sweet chocolate to refine the sense of taste".

She is very much aware that the beauty of affection isn't bound to the unremarkable subjugation. Maybe it is generally energetic and flourishes in the core of people, "in all seasons hot or cold," and it has an everlasting ability to mellow even the hardest heart. Without a doubt, the vibe of affection honours individuals.

Quotes

"You are part of my existence, part of myself.
You have been in every line I have ever read."

- Charles Dickens.

Contents

Melody to Myrtle

An Enigmatic Diary

I am my innermost life and the emotions of someone.
What's the best characteristic about me?
I never pass criticism! I am the unseen yet vital support.
Write your heart out without any worries in the world.
Images imprinted in my psyche are never forgotten.
Is there anyone who complains about me?
No, I don't think you will. I prefer to remain unnoticed.
When someone destroys me, I feel the worst.
But to many, I am a valuable treasure.
I understand how someone feels.
But who gives a damn about it?
What's published about me is significant.
I don't always appear magnificent and gorgeous.
And not my appearance. I'm not a human,
After all, I am An Enigmatic Diary.

Song of Sea of Love in Cup of Cappuccino

I feel his love in a cup of cappuccino,
The room–when I'm sleepy,
Warmth makes me heart abloom.
At times, he rubs my feet, though I don't ask—
And gives me lotion for my dried hands.
He tries his best to meet my every task,
And when we fight, he shows he understands.
But does he feel the love I have for him?
My sea of love for him is to the brim,
But, knowing the linguaphile is so tough.
Our words of affirmation–love you;
In darling buds of nights were—one of the little things that,
Prove hearts are true.

Cute Conversations

Turquoise
"If you promise to kiss me, I promise to dream you",
As sweet and cool.
"Hoping you savour a dark without my snore",
As to parched lips in the lagoon.

Ethereal
"Time to ride the rainbow in Purple Island",
When the floral asleep in the universe.
"Music is the moonlight in the gloomy night",
To only brook that creeps.

Turquoise
"Twilight is the time the pupil opens up."
But, something sugary as morning is bright.
"I will cover the stars and blacken the clouds."
So, the heavens ere out the lights.

Ethereal
"Dispelling of foggy happiness in truth",
And from their misty cushions rise.
"Showers are the gateway to peace".
Virgin flowers partially open their eyes.

O 'Vernal

The vernal brilliance of my darling's lips
Was closed like a red rose upon my mouth,
His voice was more extravagant than the mumbling leaves,
His adoration around me than the mid-year air.
Five hours snared in the curl's cry,
Lay my dearest twixt my blissful bosoms.
The wood pigeon her divine, moving speech;
But honey to my happy and singing heart.

Red Rose
"Pecks planted with love grow beautiful memories",
Mouth shut and petals scoured her lips.
"Pinch the pink rosebud",
Set down your joyful chest on my ecstasy.

Dove
"Illuminate our hearts with a deep sense of contentment."
Crushed in between the smell of coffee.
"The words of kindness are more healing to a drooping heart",
As long as I'm living, my baby, you'll be.

Words of Affection

I taste them as they bubble,
That it is so gorgeous–
To have the colder time of the year,
Sun leak deftly all the rage—
Pastel pink, becoming flushed,
A sentiment,
A sluggish dance,
The daystar,
The godly force of delicate things
Smacking them elegantly unobtrusively,
While all that around sings:
The coffee, the daisy, the steam.
Furthermore,
I find there could be—
Three unique words for affection:
Warmth, enthusiasm, home.

Bubble
"Adam's apple is full of golden dreams",
My love for you is fragile, fleeting like soap.
"Love makes your soul crawl over cupids",
To you, my heart kicks a bounce of wink.

Warmth
"Be my pillow, I'll be your blanket",
Your warmth still feels alive.
"You should be cuddled and often",
A tongue wobbled around my chin.

Daisy

"It folds your heart and takes you everywhere",
I and you steam in the world of love.
"Give me more caresses; satisfy my hungriness."
Love you tenderly, enchanting my sweat on you.

Home

"Inside of ourselves lays home",
I am safe in his arms, a pure place.
"Outside of the comfort zone—magic happens",
You're my serenity, as now and always.

Sea

Love, a second drop thy hands ;
Night inside, my spirit grows.
With that gloomy, dark hair,
Cover your pretty faces in milk—rose.
Coral kisses violate not
When the spirit is touched with thought,
Then, scorching looks are out.
Hover–over those deep–blue wells like a settling dove.
Murkiness lights up; pomp of foam,
Silvering flees the pushed sea.

Night

In the tweet, hazy hours,
by this flower treasure house.
With their springtime honey-fed
happy mouths and soft cheeks.
Flushed with love's rosy sunlight,
many girl's lips were ruby red.
Rosy lips of numerous a kid,
Carefree found slopes of euphoria.
Ruby–directed through a kiss,
To the sweet roadways of delight.

Cuckoo

Furthermore, that profound light of paradise over the trees,
Alert mid leaves that dream in brilliant harmony.
Sweet bird song, but the cuckoo's voice is heard most often
Dream-like showers.
Hints of the arousing scene, the year's increment,
New youth in the clouded human heart.

The Unspoken Rhyme

My life is then squandered farthest,
My melody, however inactive breeze,
Since you only find,
In this woven abundance of rhyme.
A carcanet of sound,
A cloud of lovely words?
Harsh figures with harsh music?
Uncouth bird's voices?
Nor Shelley's verse torment,
Nor Keats, the artist without peer.
I, by the Indian waters huge,
Seen the wizardry of the past,
Also, on the oaten line I play,
Twisted reverberations of a prior day,
I concentrated on Nature like a book.
Men rack for implications; however, I find,
No rubric in the red rose,
No upright in the mumbling wind,
No message in the snow.
No messenger of the sun am I,
Yet, in a twilight vale, A chestnut songbird.

Mute and White

How is she able to read these lifeless lines,
O letter, mute and white.
With no fire to prove it,
When others' passionate hearts exceed.
Caressing her sweet name with words of love?

Unused Life

My life is wasted like a light on fire
Inside a single house unused,
Albeit the spirit he stays with loses paradise.
I burn, and I have no idea why ;
I am forbidden from rebelling
And sink to hell without success.

Mistake

Twists came to you with traces of honey;
Day revealed a brighter hope
Than this dim thought shielded your heart,
And called you far away.
You made a mistake.
Must I then, at that point, rage, develop sick,
With tormented vanity and thinking it love,
Mistake with severe names my woman's will
Fouling thy snow white picture,
O my pigeon?
Isn't thy kiss enough,
However, only one forever to live upon?

Center of Living

The New Year brings us many blessings,
But the gifts of the old world were three:
The camouflage of the chameleon, the wine of Dionysus
And Shrikhand in Sicily. "Wine enters through the mouth,
Love the eyes; I rise the glass of tune,
Look at you and sigh" The centre of living.
Best, most seasoned, musicale,
If, at the end of the forward effort,
These, Life's first, also proved to be the best.
Long be thy days in downpour and daylight,
Frequently thy spring rekindle,
Delighting thy mother's heart with thy excellence,
Blossom like carrying out thy delicate responsibility,
To be cherished and sprout,
O dear kid soul, our adored and appreciated,
For this thy days had birth,
Like some delicate bloom on a dim stone entrance,
To improve and flush with adolescence unfading,
The maturing earth.

Earth's Carnival

World's joy, spring's pleasantness, music's appeal
Exist in my arm;
I am Mastered on my knees,
Present earth and future heaven are here.
Open thy rose petals, falling down,
Furthermore, thy heart reveals.
Oh my joy, give me your fragrance,
The aroma fills the entire night.
Thou had and I having earth
Open for our pleasure. Blossoms dropping on us
From charmed trees, the carnival of the breeze,
For me—since I hold their Circe white,
Sovereign of their glee.
Wanton, thou shalt know at last a chain
Golden to restrain.
Not a moment of you will get away from my kiss,
Hostage made to rapture, Not a short breath,
But love will take her away with his ecstasy,
Let your whole body be a harp of wonderful joy,
toyed with desire.

He Loves me, Loves me not

In the realm of drunken vows and vacant gaze,
Where secrets dwell, and bed sheets interweave,
Halfway between, where love's elusive maze,
Reveals the truth, the depths we both perceive.

For underneath the surface, whispers lay,
Unveiling layers, hidden mysteries true.
I've glimpsed a soul transcending what you say,
A flawed perfection only I pursue.

Yet, in this fragile bond, our bodies fought,
A passionate dance, but lacking the key,
To bridge the void, the chasm left untaught,
Now, my rib's rift, a wound for all to see.

But, dear, your love resides within my core,
Though not the girl you wished for, I'm loved and more.

Your Hearts Unleash

In tender hands, my heart found solace true,
You let it dwell, a home inside your own,
As gentle as a rose, a flower's hue,
But petals fell, now left bone dry, alone.

Each petal plucked, a piece of me undone,
The thorns remain, a painful memory,
And now, a vacant gaze, where love had shone,
Did you, dear one, ever truly care for me?

Within this sonnet's frame, my words do dwell,
Short versus capturing this bitter truth,
The ache of love, a story I must tell,
A fragile heart, now worn and stripped of youth.

Yet still, I wonder, did you ever care,
Or was my heart a burden you could bear?

I’m Your Pumpkin

Summer solstice stings the city of Philadelphia skyline after an oil refinery explosion turns clouds to lanterns as you watch your newborn scream, her body pulsing purple from needle pricks they stuck and locked again, draining her garnet-apple heels to ensure that your veins hadn't ravaged hers, the lethal mixing of opposing blood types your mother feared would render you infertile after your first child. But you don't fear what your bodies can do to one another; you don't fear the red or yellow you can see igniting her skin, the bilirubin increasing, the amber glow encircling her iris, the danger to her body caused by yours. Don't breathe, and tell acquaintances from out of the area that the air is poisonous. But you additionally understand there's no escape from what's above the
skin or what's beneath. A decade before you were born, Ukraine's sky was likewise radioactive, and you imagined a bear ate the stars, ripped apart its name: Chornobyl, Chernobyl, black agony, envisioned mother's consuming in stupor when light fell through the bear's mouth onto their children's, imagined how some shut their vents, blinds, and extending uneasy of flying ash, constellations doused dark, and more terrified of what's been rendered invisible. However, everybody who inhaled suffered the same way, with bear blood slowly boiling from within and generations of sterile women and children trapped in space. Here, with your baby, not forty-eight hours old, you tear her maiden name apart, René Luray, a woman who oars a crooked river, a cavern, the heavens, one who draws your body into memory. Her hot, prepared mouth reaches for your star-cracked nipples. Remy opens his bold, tea-candle eyes. Gulps colostrums, lively, blood-laced, to safeguard her from

millennia of blazon oxygen she's unaware is already igniting inside her.

One Person Matters

In the end, only one person matters: the one that you imagine when you're away from the insanity, the one who comes to mind when you sit in peace, and the one you perceive when you close your eyes.

Love-Cushion

Speak with me, lean on me,
express to me everything
that worries you,
dive into me,
dissolve into me,
the love that will keep you cosy,
let it all smash into me,
because I'm here to help cushion your fall.

Seasons of Change

"Our love sounded like seasons of change.
I longed for you in autumn,
whilst you were already in the fall".

Essence

Most meaningful meetings,
happen during a cup of coffee,
is the essence of the heart?

Blew

I blew kisses softly into my words
Knowing that they will reach you soon,
and once they do,
I'm hopeful they will remain.

Dazzling Hues

Your love is like rainbows and unicorns, dazzling my eyes
with stunning hues.
However, when I attempt to extend out to touch these
feelings, I just catch empty signals,
I've been fantasizing about illusory meadows and horses,
things that I haven't encountered or seen,
It is time to awaken from this appeal, sleep and cease this
make-believe vision.

Lost in yours

Even before you touched me,
I belong to you!
All you had to do was look into my eyes.
You pierce my soul; I am half hope
I have loved none but you!
He never knew that I loved him.
It's not because he is cuter; he is more than I am!
And I will kiss every single scar on your body to remind
That love doesn't hurt!
Each time my man looks into me,
He is searching himself, for he knows already that he is a part
of me in all souls!
As pieces of clouds dissolve in sunlight, likewise
My happiness will indulge in your eyesight!

My eyes met many eyes, but lost in yours,
I lost in yours, but truth be told,
I don't want a way to find out!

The Anonymous

Mine: What do you want?
Yours: I want a small palace to be built inside your heart
Only known to you.
Mine: Will you be my swan?
Yours: I will be there as a listener when you feel like running away,
So complain to me!
Mine: Will it be another journey, maybe?
Yours: Love is binding us to eternity, so let's journey together.
Mine: What blocked you?
Yours: The roses fell from the moon and wiped my face,
Just like your hands, so miss me every time.

Flawless

I tracked down an adoration,
for me, Sweetheart,
Simply make a plunge and take cues from me,
All things considered,
I tracked down a young lady,
Lovely and sweet,
Goodness,
I never realized you were the,
somebody sitting tight for me,
Because we were simply kids,
When we experience passionate feelings for,
Not understanding what it was,
I won't surrender you this time,
In any case, sweetheart,
Simply kiss me slow,
Your heart is all I own.
What's more, in your eyes,
you're holding mine,
Child, I'm moving in obscurity,
With you between my arms,
Shoeless on the grass,
Paying attention to our main tune.
All things considered,
I tracked down a lady,
More grounded than anybody I know
She shares my fantasies,
I trust that at some time or another, I'll share her home
I tracked down a sweetheart,
to convey something beyond my insider facts
To convey love,

To convey offspring of our own.

Daffodils

I'm tinting colours to me—about you,
You're my dream,
What's more, our affection is vast, out of this multitude of blossoms,
I check you out,
So keep me near your lovely heart,
Furthermore, I'll hold you through everything,
Yellow petals bloom, love flows,
Daffodils kiss.
I love it when you're simply near,
You are my daffodils between our lips,
You're the number one of my blossoms.
Discussions we have the entire night under our heavenly bodies,
It's perpetual, like we've hung tight for our entire lives, feels right,
So normal, like when the sun is breathing on its blossoms,
(Breathing on its blossoms).
Our blossoms sprout in spring,
I want to give my admission, but I know there's no assurance.
In the spring, our flowers grow,
I'm prepared to admit that you are a gift to me.

Rarest to Millions

In the vast expanse of the garden's embrace,
There are millions of roses, a dazzling display,
But amidst the bloom and the fragrant haze,
Your presence, a lavender, steals my gaze.

Rare and exquisite, you stand apart,
A breath of fresh air, a work of art,
In a world of abundance, you shine bright,
A precious gem in the soft moonlight.

Your essence, a whisper in the breeze,
A melody that puts my heart at ease,
Among the roses, you bloom with grace,
A lavender beauty in this sacred space.

So let the garden flourish, let it thrive,
For in your presence, it truly comes alive,
There are millions of roses, but you, my dear,
Are a rarity, a treasure so near.

Signs of Love

In the signs of love that softly glow,
Whispers of care in gestures small,
A gentle touch, a kind hello,
In every moment, love stands tall.

From grocery runs to heartfelt deeds,
Expressions of love in words so sweet,
A helping hand in times of need,
Guiding each other, hearts to meet.

The simple acts that show we care,
In every gesture, love is found,
Together, in the moments we share,
In every sign, love does abound.

In open hearts and open doors,
In tender moments, love resides,
A bond that strengthens and endures,
In signs of love, our hearts confide.

A symphony of love's embrace,
In every action, big or small,
In each sweet gesture, we can trace
The signs of love that bind us all.

In every action, big or small,
Love's presence echoes through it all,
A gentle whisper, a silent call,
Guiding us never to fall.

This Made Me Think About You

Hands to Lovers

They stand in the silent silence of expectation.
Would you kindly stand, ladies and gentlemen?
Every scar on an instrument's strings is
evidence of the journey
A powerful attraction bringing two spirits together

Heart blue, heart borrowed, entwined in the embrace of love
In the embrace of their lover, everything
works out for the best.
Vows delivered with emotion
Overly theatrical and true, a pledge to cherish and
honour for all eternity.

The dirtiest jokes whispered together.
A connection bound by understanding and humor
There is a place assigned for two at each table.
In this soul-dancing, they discover their beat.

They stroll hand in hand, lovers to lovers.
Bound by an unfathomable love,
Through all of life's highs and lows and turns
Their story is written in the stars,
A love to stand the test of time.

Spellbinding

In the alchemy of glances, we find
The elixir—a catalyst in the mundane,
A bus missed, stars unwittingly aligned,
We fall like leaves and surrender to the wind.

In the silence of an elevator's climb,
Or the shared gaze across a history book's spine,
We are but atoms in a vast design,
Drawn together, inexplicably entwined.

In the small hours when the world sleeps tight,
Souls crave company to share the night,
A touch, a whisper, against the lonely tide,
We find harbour in each other's light.

Coca-Cola eyes, fizzing with life's lure,
A glance, a smile, becomes the cure
To the ennui that time assures,
We fall in love to feel and endure.

On a Wednesday barstool, we sit, a pair of ghosts,
Finding solace as the world toasts,
To the lonely hearts, the love posts,
In each other's eyes, we coast.

Trembling hands, seeking a steady shore,
Find in another's grip something more,
A strength borrowed, a shared folklore,
We fall in love with the hope we store.

For the child's dream, the artist's drive,
For Springsteen's anthems that make us feel alive,
For Patti's quest, the friend she'd derive,
We fall in love, to create, to contrive.
In courage, in fear, a leap into the night,
Believing in love's endless flight,
We fall, we rise, in love's sweet light,
Because, perhaps, it's our only right.

Mousy girls and memories of a man's embrace,
We love in defiance of time and space,
Not always a choice but a saving grace,
We fall in love with the human race.

Ecstasy of Connection

In the quiet language of glances exchanged,
Where eyes lock, and the world's clamor fades,
We converse in the hush of shared sight,
An intimacy is woven in the warp and weft of light.
Smirks ripple across the room's vast sea,
Playful conspiracies, just you and me.
Eyebrows arch, a silent ballet,
Sketching stories we dare not say.

In nimble wit and verbal dance,
We parry, thrust—the sweet advance
Of minds that spar with gentle jest,
Finding in banter a place to rest.

The melody that stirs the air,
Whispers, "You're the reason it's there."
A song, a memory, just a tune,
Binding like threads of a cocoon.

Legs touch, a spark beneath the guise
Of accident—a connection that belies
The casual brush, the feigned retreat,
A silent confession, subtly sweet.
And there, amidst the throng's loud stare,
We dance as if we're unaware
Of any others, our rhythm found
In movements small yet profound.
In jest, a tease, a playful poke,
A bubble of laughter soon evoked.
"I saved you space," a simple phrase,

Yet, in it, a universe of care is encased.
Silences that hum with unspoken words,
comfort in the quiet, where hearts are heard.
Together, we slumber, a couch our domain,
In dreams, we converse, entwined in the refrain.

Sorrow whisper, "I'm so sorry," sincerely,
a salve to the soul when one is near.
Hope, like dawn, begins to unfurl,
a fragile bloom in a weary world.

In the minutiae, our affection is sown,
in the little things, true love is shown.
Inside jokes, a secret lexicon,
a language of two, a lifelong bond.

Appreciation, a silent hymn,
trust exchanged on a mutual whim.
"You're my best friend," a fortress built,
a sanctuary from all guilt.

Crying alone, a red light's caress,
the car a confessional for the heart's distress.
Bonds forged in the most unlikely places
dive bar hearts with empathic faces.

Benefit of doubt, a gift we give,
the grace through which the flawed can live.
Second chances, a precious coin,
in the currency of life, we join.
Surrender to laughter, deep and true,
a tide that pulls me back to you.
The serendipity of a call about to make,
our lives, it seems, are at stake.

Books shared, margins filled with thought,
the scribbles of souls seeking what's sought.
A stumble, a catch, a steadying hand,
intimacy that doesn't demand.

Secrets spilled, a trust bequeathed,
in hushed tones where breaths are sheathed.
First hugs, tight and warm,
a prelude to storms, a coming swarm.

A kiss, a goodbye, a silent pact,
a moment cherished, a final act.
"I understand," the softest shield,
in empathy, our bond is sealed.
Safety, a harbour from the storm,
in your presence, my heart is warm.
Alignment, a sense of coming home,
in your eyes, I am never alone.
The unspoken promise of something more,
a belief in us, an open door.
In the quiet moments, the subtle plays,
our love, a dance through life's maze.

Epiphany of Soul

In the quiet gallery of my day,
I stand, a silent observer,
caught in the candid frame of your gaze,
my cheeks bloom with the secret garden
of an unspoken crush,
a transient masterpiece of blush.
The night whispers in a crescent moon smile,
a soft arc of understanding,
that curves in the dark like a knowing child,
watching as hearts fumble with the language
of glances that linger a second too long,
a silent sonnet, a wordless song.

Eyes, deep pools brimming with unshed rain,
hold the gravity of a thousand oceans,
I meet them not as a voyeur of pain,
but as a guardian of the moment's rawness,
in a silent pact, we share the weight,
our gaze, a cradle for their heartache.

A stranger's words, like a serendipitous breeze,
flutter the fabric of an ordinary day,
their compliment threads into my seams,
a stitch in the tapestry of self-belief,
a small act weaving strangers into kin,
as serenity blooms from without to within.
"I love you, too," the echo of our syncopation,
a refrain that sings of certainty and doubt,
a melody of equal parts elation
and the quiet terror of living without,

our voices, imperfect, the notes we fumble,
a duet in the key of being humble.

Singing out of key, our anthem in the car,
a symphony of inside jokes and laughter,
each misnote a testament to who we are,
discordant harmonies we'll chase after,
for in these moments, love is a playful tease,
a dance of joyous, off-key melodies.

A trusted eye peruses my soul's draft,
the scribbles, the errors, the crossed-out lines,
my best friend, keeper of my fore and aft,
reads the truth between my clumsy rhymes,
in their hands, my fledgling words take flight,
in their smile, my world finds its light.

Old love's texts, a digital reliquary,
kept in the vault just in case,
a hopeful heart's contradictory diary,
where past and potential interlace,
a cache of words that may never come to pass,
but hope clings to the screen of looking glass.

"How are you, really?" the question delves,
past the facade of "I'm fine" and its ilk,
an invitation to reveal ourselves,
to let down walls, to share the ilk
of our true state, a compassionate plea,
to step out from our own debris.

At a funeral, hands reach across the divide,
a silent language of shared sorrow,
a lifeline in the ceremonial tide,

the touch that says, "I'm here today, tomorrow,"
a grasp that anchors, that says, "You're not alone,"
in the language more felt than known.

Reaching out first after the discord of a fight,
the outstretched hand after the storm,
a bridge built in the aftermath of spite,
a gesture, a small but transformative form,
an olive branch extended in the silence,
the first step back to the alliance.

A realization as poignant as it is stark,
our love story's final, bittersweet verse,
a journey's end, a ship that leaves its mark,
sailing from harbour with our course reversed,
the conclusion reached, not with fanfare or roar,
but the quiet closing of a door.

"You remind me of home," those words, a key
to the map of our shared history,
a whisper that unlocks the memory,
the sentiment as comforting as it is heady,
a reminder of roots, of belonging, of lore,
the feeling of warmth at the core.

Promises whispered beneath the veiled night,
vows that dance on the edge of breath,
frail as spider silk, yet holding tight,
entwining futures, fears, life, and death,
the hushed oaths that lovers dare to speak,
the bond that both fortifies and makes weak.

Returning their things while they're out of sight,
a ritual of closure, a silent farewell,

the final act of love once bright,
each object a story, a memory to quell,
a chapter ends as I leave behind
the tangible remnants of a love resigned.

A third chance, a risk, a leap of faith,
hope's stubborn flame flickers anew,
forgiveness' path, a delicate wraith,
trusting once more in the promise of true,
a heart's resilience, the courage to mend,
the belief that love can ascend.

Surrendering the need to be right,
in the grand bazaar of human interaction,
a concession, a release, a relinquishing of fight,
finding peace in the act of subtraction,
a quiet victory not in winning,
but in the growth of a new beginning.

Faith without reason, a blind man's sight,
a belief in the unseen, the yet-to-come,
a starless navigation through the night,
a conviction that cannot be undone,
trust in the journey, though the path is unknown.

Charm of Tiny Delights

In whispers soft, at two, the text takes flight,
"Home safe?" it asks through the digital embrace.
Upon the floor, our hearts converse till light,
In honesty, our souls are exposed, face to face.

The photo shared a likeness true and kind,
No vanity shall breach the trust we've spun.
In silence shared, a language of the mind,
An eyebrow speaks a thousand words in one.

In code, we cloak the names of fleeting loves,
A secret dance of glances, soft and sly.
In tandem thought, our patience gently proves,
A tapestry of trust, woven high.

Through apps, our chatter flits, a ceaseless stream,
Yet silence speaks the volume of our dream.

For in each jest, a thread of care is spun,
A soft tease masks the depth of what we mean.
In garb aligned, we face the night as one,
A duo carved from the same storied scene.

An oath we take, "This stays 'tween you and I,"
A vault of hopes and dreams we both shall keep.
Through time's cruel march, our bond will not untie,
For in our hearts, the roots have grown too deep.

To kin, not blood, yet cherished all the same,
An aunt to theirs, a role I proudly claim.

In every life, our friendship shall ignite,
A constant flame, undimmed by doubt or blame.

This sonnet hums the tune of platonic love,
A melody that fits us like a glove.

A Sonnet of Platonic Passion

Upon the morn, the sun's caress alights,
Its golden touch, a warm and gentle kiss,
A herald to the day that it ignites,
A tender balm, a prelude to bliss.

Within the woven words of books, I find
A passage that, like a whispered secret, speaks,
A mirror to the soul, to heart, to mind,
A friend who knows the truth my spirit seeks.

In poetry, one line, a simple thread,
Invites my gaze to worlds unseen, unthought,
A new perspective on the path I tread,
A lesson in the tapestry it's wrought.

A lyric stirs, awakens depths within,
A melody where lost emotions spin.

The tails of dogs, a joyous wiggle dance,
A script of ink that flows in graceful lines,
In service, hearts connect and take the chance,
To mend the world with a love that intertwines.

A city new, with streets I've yet to roam,
A freshened view, a purpose to renew,
With watercolours, even clumsy home
Is found in strokes of chromatic hue.

The concert's cusp, when lights descend tonight,
And hearts in harmony, together leap,

The thunderous pulse, a shared and pure delight,
A symphony of souls, a boundless sweep.

In rebuilding life, each brick and each new tone,
A language rich through which my heart has grown.

In summer's pool, I swim, the water's hug,
And dance alone, where rhythm is my guide,
A sense of "alive," a feeling snug,
In every act, in every heartfelt stride.

As life unfolds, a sonnet to impart,
The love, the joy, the growth that we achieve,
Each line a step, each word a beat of heart,
In every breath, the art of how we weave.

Alive in dance, in song, in hue, in script,
In tails that wag, in cities yet unzipped,
Alive in all, the sun's first morning dipped,
A sonnet scribed, a life in passion dipped.

Craving the Comfort

I'm out of my head, a carousel spinning,
Unhinged from the axis, a world all beginning.
The space where logic and wild dreams collide,
A tangle of whispers where secrets abide.

Out of my mind, oh, I tumble and soar,
Through the vastness of wanting and yearning for more.
The night's velvet touch is a siren's soft plea,
In this realm of the senseless, you're gravity to me.

If you let me, I'll be a comet set free,
A blaze in the dark, what I'm meant to be.
No longer tethered in orbit's confine,
I'll dance through the cosmos, your hand clasped in mine.

Out of my dress, a petal unwound,
Into your arms, where all fears are drowned.
Tonight is our canvas; let passion ignite,
In the stroke of your touch, in the depth of the night.

Yeah, I'm lost without it, that spark in your gaze,
A lighthouse in storms, the sun's warming rays.
The compass you are in my sea of disquiet,
Steers me through chaos, through silence, through riot.

Feels like I'm always wait in', a statue in rain,
For the brush of your lips to release me from pain.
Each second without you, an unending mile,
Each tick of the clock, a stone in the pile.

I need you to come get me, unravel the threads,
That tie me to solitude, to echoes and dreads.
Be the artist, the sculptor, who frees my form,
From the marble of doubts, cold and forlorn.

Out of my head and into your arms tonight,
Let's dissolve in the ether; let's take our flight.
No more the waiting, no more the fight,
In the cradle of dusk, 'til the dawn's early light.

Tonight tonight, the world is our stage,
And life is a book, and we are the page.
Together, we've written a story so bright,
Out of my head and into your arms tonight.

Amidst the downpour, still, I stand and pine,
A marble figure beneath the weeping sky.
I long for the soft touch of lips like wine,
To kiss away the ache I can't deny.

In the Stillness of Night

In the dim-lit hush of the cinema's embrace,
We whisper during movies, our words a gentle trace
Of thoughts exchanged in shadows, a clandestine dance,
Our murmurs interlaced in a silent, shared romance.

We laugh over inside jokes,
A secret lexicon of mirth only we invoke.
In laughter, our souls undress,
Revealing the tender chaos of our togetherness.

We sing off-key on purpose,
Our voices are soaring, gloriously worthless.
Notes dancing in the air, carefree and unbound,
A symphony of imperfection, a love profound.

We have a secret language,
A tapestry of glances, gestures, a silent homage
To the world, we've built within the world we know,
A cocoon of understanding, where only we go.

We eat too much takeout,
Cardboard boxes our tableware, there's no doubt.
Savouring flavours from afar in our shared space,
A feast not just of food but of grace.

We share everything we can,
Our dreams, our fears, the entire span
Of who we are, laid bare, intertwined,
In the open book of our hearts, you'll find.

We are best friends and lovers,
In us, the line between the two hovers,
Blurring into a single entity, a fusion complete,
In every triumph, every trial, we meet.

We are perfectly imperfect,
Our flaws, our quirks, we do not reject.
They are the brushstrokes in our masterpiece,
A portrait of love that will never cease.

We are how I want to be forever,
In this dance of ours, so clever,
Where time is a melody, and space a gentle caress,
In your arms, in our world, in shared happiness.

The world spins on in a muted whirl,
As love blossoms unfurl,
In the stillness of night, under the star's bright necklace,
Time pauses, a moment of perfect, tranquil symphony.

Love Is an Endless Dance

Love is the gentle drape of warmth upon your
chilled and dreaming form,
A blanket's tender weight that speaks in silent, woven terms.
It whispers through the threads and fibres,
"You are not alone,"
And in its cozy grasp, the world's sharp
edges are softly honed.

Love is the brush of lips on foreheads in the
quiet, dusky room,
A benediction, soft as prayer that keeps the
lurking fears entombed.
It's in the simple, caring gestures, "Take your
meds," a daily chant,
A lifeline thrown across the chasm where the
darker shadows haunt.

"Put your seatbelt on," they say, a mantra of
protective care,
A string of words that binds us closer,
an unseen ribbon in the air.
It's in the long embraces offered, a haven from the storm,
A port of solace for weary souls, a place
where hearts are warmed.

Love is delving into pasts, into wounds that time has scored,
It's touching scars and feeling tremors,
a shared and silent chord.
It's the bravery of broaching topics laden with old fears,
A commitment to the journey through the

laughter and tears.

Love is the one who speaks first after anger's bitter taste,
Who understands the need for space, yet
never leaves a void to waste.
"Let's fix it together," a promise made of steel and light,
A pact to face the broken pieces, to make the crooked right.

"Did you eat?" the question lingers,
care wrapped in daily bread,
A knowledge of each preference, each desire softly read.
It's in the sharing of the mundane, the
books, the songs, the nights,
In every cherished favourite, the world is set to rights.

Love is the lame joke cracked, a lifeline to a smile,
The effort was made to lift the spirit and ease the weary mile.
It's in the echo of your sorrow, in the mirror of their pain,
A testament to connection, a bond that shall remain.

Love is the respect for lines drawn for
boundaries set in place,
An honouring of the sacred ground, a giving of due space.
It's in the details memorized, the minutiae held dear,
The attentive ear to passions voiced, letting none disappear.

Love is watching eyes that sparkle, that dance with inner fire,
As they speak of all they treasure, as
they unwrap their heart's desire.
It's in the freedom to be open, to share the
hidden parts of you,
Knowing in their careful keeping,
your secrets will remain true.

To love is to stand steadfast through the trials that will come,
To be the constant in the chaos, the unyielding, beating drum.
It's in the acceptance of your being, in the
shelter of their arms,
A declaration that amidst the fray, you shall come to no harm.

Love is all of these and more, a tapestry of acts and words,
It's the flight of mundane moments,
alongside the flights of birds.
An art of presence and of giving, a dance of push and pull,
A complex, simple, wondrous thing, perpetually full.

Murmurs of Desire

Let us gather in melody, our voices entwined,
A chorus of unity, leaving none behind.
Hold fast, hold close, in the dance of the night,
Swaying to the symphony of love's tender light.

Through the pulse of rhythm, spirits freely roam,
In the laughter of a tune that guides us home.
Hand in hand, we step, a serenade so sweet,
As love's harmonious path unfolds beneath our feet.

Wander with me to the town's heart, where blooms blush,
Their crimson whispers in a hush.
A bouquet for mother, petals of the deepest red,
A token of affection, a word unsaid.

Her smile, a sunburst, a joy unveiled,
In the simple act of love, so deeply inhaled.
For in that giving, happiness takes flight,
A moment was shared, and a day turned bright.

Else, with friends, let's lose ourselves in time,
Capture the now in frames, in joy so sublime.
Dressed in our finest, we laugh, and we weave,
A tapestry of memories that we'll never leave.

But if solitude calls, and the heart seeks to roam,
Gift yourself the world – let your spirit comb.
Adorn yourself in self-love, a treasure so rare,
Spread the love wide, let it touch the air.

For, in the end, it's love that we sing, that we wear,
A force that binds, an ultimate dare.
To dance, to give, to cherish, to hold,
In a song of love, forever bold.

Crimson Kisses

In this ink-draped night, where stars forget to gleam,
Let me love you, not in fragments,
Not in the scattered whispers of a dream,
But wholly, with the full weight of my being.

I shall play with your tresses, each strand a storyline,
Unraveling the knots of your day,
Each twist and curl falling in line,
As my fingers dance their worries away.

No barriers left, just the space we consume,
I'll draw you near, into my embrace,
Where the world outside cannot resume,
And time surrenders to our pace.

Upon your cheeks, my fingertips will roam,
Tracing the paths of laughter and sorrow,
Fondling each memory that has found a home,
In the canvas of your skin, where our past and future borrow.

Warm kisses I will plant, a tender gardener am I,
Sowing seeds of affection with each caress,
Sprouting blooms of passion beneath the sigh,
Of our mingled breaths, in silent confess.

Here, love swells, a tide that knows no retreat,
It urges our souls to a boundless flight,
Where the heart beats a rhythm, both fierce and sweet,
A symphony of desire that fills the night.

Let love grow deep within, an unspoken vow,
An anchor in the tumult, an unwavering glow,
As we unite, our spirits entwined, here and now,
In a world where only true lovers know.